NATIONAL GEOGRAPHIC

Missions and Ranchos

Early California Life

Gare Thompson

PICTURE CREDITS
Cover, 10-11 Fine Arts Museum of San Francisco; page 1 Gary Geiger; pages 2-3 Pajaro Valley Historical Association; pages 4, 7, 11, 17, 21, 25 (borders), Londie G. Padelesky; page 4 (bottom) California Historical Society; pages 4 (top), 6 (middle), 6 (bottom left), 6 (top right), 16-17, 22-23, 26-27 The Granger Collection, NY; page 6 (top left) Peter Newark's American Pictures; page 6 (bottom right) Getty Images; pages 7, 20-21 North Wind Pictures; pages 8-9, 10, 18-19, 24-25, 30-31, 38-39 The Bancroft Library, University of California, Berkeley; pages 12-13, 36-37 Los Angeles County Museum of Natural History; page 12 Ben Klaffke; pages 14, 32-33 Oakland Museum; pages 22, 27 Dennis Wyszynski/The Monterey History and Art Association, Casa Serrano Collection; page 26 Thomas Walker; page 28 Archivo General de Indias, Seville; page 28-29 Garzoli Gallery; page 31 Craig Lovell; page 32-33 Thomas Gilcrease Institute; page 40 Peabody Museum.

Produced through the worldwide resources of the National Geographic Society, John M. Fahey, Jr., President and Chief Executive Officer; Gilbert M. Grosvenor, Chairman of the Board; Nina D. Hoffman, Executive Vice President and President, Books and Education Publishing Group.

PREPARED BY NATIONAL GEOGRAPHIC SCHOOL PUBLISHING
Ericka Markman, Senior Vice President and President, Children's Books and Education Publishing Group; Steve Mico, Vice President, Editorial Director; Marianne Hiland, Executive Editor; Anita Schwartz, Project Editor, Jim Hiscott, Design Manager; Kristin Hanneman, Illustrations Manager; Diana Bourdrez, Picture Editor; Matt Wascavage, Manager of Publishing Services; Sean Philpotts, Production Manager.

Manufacturing and Quality Management
Christopher A. Liedel, Chief Financial Officer; Phillip L. Schlosser, Director; Clifton M. Brown, Manager.

PROGRAM DEVELOPMENT
Gare Thompson Associates, Inc.

ART DIRECTION
Dan Banks, Project Design Company

CONSULTANTS/REVIEWERS
Dr. Margit E. McGuire, School of Education, Seattle University, Seattle, Washington
Carol Berkin, Professor of History, Baruch College and CUNY Graduate Center
Peter Uhrowczik, author, *The Burning of Monterey: The 1818 Attack on California by the Privateer Bouchard*

BOOK DEVELOPMENT
Nieman Inc.

BOOK DESIGN
Steven Curtis Design, Inc.

PICTURE EDITING AND MANAGEMENT
Paula McLeod, Worth a Thousand Words, Inc.

MAP DEVELOPMENT AND PRODUCTION
Russ Charpentier

Published by the National Geographic Society
Washington, D.C. 20036-4688

Product No. 4J41742

ISBN-13: 978-0-7922-4548-3
ISBN-10: 0-7922-4548-2

Printed in Canada

11 10 09 08 07 06
10 9 8 7 6 5 4

Table of Contents

INTRODUCTION	Early California	4
CHAPTER 1	Life on the Rancho	7
CHAPTER 2	The Festival	11
CHAPTER 3	Visitors Arrive	17
CHAPTER 4	Uprising and Escape	21
CHAPTER 5	Battling the Pirates	25
CHAPTER 6	The Governor Visits	33
EPILOGUE		38
GLOSSARY		40

Early California

Many of the earliest Spanish settlements in what is now California began in the late 1700s and early 1800s as **missions**. Spanish missions included a church, living quarters, and farmlands. Their purpose was to spread Christianity among the Native Americans. Usually, there was a nearby fort, or **presidio**, where Spanish soldiers lived. These troops provided protection for the mission. A **pueblo**, or small town, sometimes grew up near a mission.

Father Junípero Serra, a Spanish priest, founded the first mission in California at San Diego in 1769. He and other priests were sent by Spain to convert the Native Americans to Christianity. They also taught them farming and other skills.

Junípero Serra

However, the Indians did not understand the Spanish way of life. Many of them did not want to become Christians. Often, the soldiers used force to make them live and work at the missions.

By 1823, there were 21 missions along the coast of California. Two years earlier, Mexico had won its freedom from Spain and had begun to govern California. As more Mexican settlers moved there, they wanted land to create **ranchos**, or large farms. In 1834, the Mexican government began to take land from the missions and gave it to these settlers. The ranchero families grew wheat and other crops and raised cattle. By 1838, there were many large ranchos in California. At this time, Monterey was one of the most important towns in the Mexican province of Alta California. It had been the province's capital until 1835.

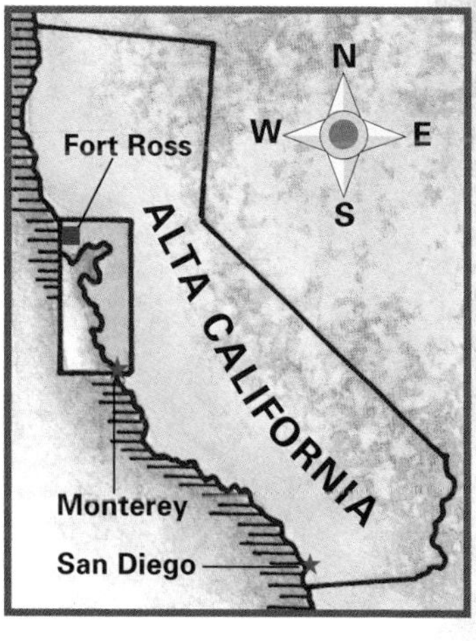

Father Serra founding Carmel Mission in 1770

MEET THE DELGADO FAMILY

In 1838, the Delgado family owns a rancho near Monterey. They grow grain, fruit, and vegetables and raise cattle and sheep. Their distant cousin, Padre Ramón, has made a long journey from Mexico to visit them. He had been a priest at the Mission San Carlos Borromeo de Carmelo, called the Carmel Mission.

During his visit, Padre Ramón tells stories to the Delgado children about life at the Carmel Mission years before. He tells them of an Indian uprising and a pirate attack. The young people listen to the stories and then write them down.

The Delgados are a fictional family. Their diary and journal entries and letters tell the story of early life in California.

Father: Felipe

Son: Simón, 18

Mother: María

Daughter: Rosalinda, 17

Padre Carlos Ramón

CHAPTER 1

Life on the Rancho

The church bells ring. It is a fine summer morning. A soft breeze drifts in from the **bay**. The red roof tiles of the **adobe** church glisten in the early morning sun. The Delgado family and Padre Ramón have come to church. Padre Ramón looks around hoping to see some old friends. He greets a former presidio soldier.

After church, some ranchero families stop to chat. It is the end of summer. The men talk of the upcoming harvest. The women speak of their homes and children. Excited voices fill the air. Everyone is looking forward to the harvest festival.

Like all rancheros, the young Delgados are fine riders. Rosalinda and Simón race home in a cloud of dust. The older Delgados and Padre Ramón head more slowly back to the rancho.

From Rosalinda's diary

July 15, 1838

At last I am out of that black dress! Mama wants me to look like a proper young lady while Padre Ramón is here. I long to put on my old clothes and just ride off! I do love the stories that the padre tells. Life in California now seems dull compared to when he lived here. Padre Ramón has promised to tell more stories at the harvest festival. I hope that he does. Maybe he will be able to get Papa and Mama to tell some stories too. We have all heard how they met and fell in love, but I am sure that they must have had other adventures! Life here is too peaceful. Still, I love the brown, rolling hills that I can see from my window.

From Simón's journal

July 16, 1838

Papa worries that new settlers from the United States will try to take our land. I like the Americans I've met, but I think Papa is right to worry. Some Americans act as if California is already part of the United States.

Papa says I should become a lawyer. It is good to know the law. I like the idea. Mama just wants me to get married. Of course I will, but that can wait. The padre is not here to see me get married!

July 18, 1838
Alta California

My Dear Brother,

I send you warm greetings from California. I trust this letter finds you and your family in good health. María and the children are well.

I am tired tonight. The day was hot, and Simón and I worked hard rounding up the cattle for slaughter. We will have a great many hides to ship out of Monterey. We will have plenty of beef for ourselves and some to sell. We just leave what we do not need. The vultures, coyotes, and grizzly bears will take care of the remains.

The weather has been dry this year. The wheat crop is small, but there is enough. We will harvest it next week. Then we will ship it by oxcart to the flour mill near the river.

Simón and Rosalinda look forward to the harvest festival. I do too. It will be good to get together with the other rancheros. There will be lively music and dancing. María loves to dance. So do the children.

Your fond brother,
Felipe

From Padre Ramón's journal
July 19, 1838

It's odd being here again. So much has changed. There are many new faces. When I was at the mission, I knew everyone. Where are the Indians I taught? I know a few work for Felipe, but where are the others? I wonder if they went back to their villages. Probably they did. They kept trying to escape when I was here. I hope that they are happy now. Time to rest. All the fresh air has made me sleepy.

A Native American of early California

The people of Alta California were friendly. Early visitors often remarked on the kindness they received. Like other rancheros, Felipe Delgado worried that some visitors would want to stay. He feared that the United States would someday try to take over California.

Now Felipe and his family were looking forward to the harvest festival. It would be a time to have fun and celebrate. Soon, the Delgado house would be full of people and music, and Padre Ramón would tell his stories.

CHAPTER 2

The Festival

The workers harvested the wheat by hand. They toiled through long, hot days. Their hands blistered. Cuts and scrapes covered their arms. Slowly, the golden fields disappeared. Felipe Delgado then shipped the wheat off to be ground into flour. Workers took the last four sheaves, or cut stalks of wheat. They tied these sheaves to form a cross. Then, they marched to the church at the presidio, carrying the cross made of wheat. Church bells rang, and the priest and a group of boys greeted the procession. The priest blessed the cross of sheaves. Then, he hung it in the church. This was an old **custom**, or traditional way of doing things.

People in early California liked to get together for events such as festivals and weddings. The ranchero families lived far apart. Travel from one rancho to another was long. Most rancheros rode. The mission priests sometimes rode, but more often used a carriage pulled by mules. Some older people traveled by oxcart. Once they arrived, however, the guests stayed awhile. The celebrations might last a week or even longer. Each night, there were huge feasts, music, dancing, and storytelling.

From Rosalinda's diary
July 22, 1838

Mama has made me a beautiful skirt. I cannot wait for the dancing tonight.

Padre Ramón was showing me one of the hymn books he used to teach his Indians at the mission to sing. He looked sad. I could tell he was missing the old days.

I have to help Mama with the food. She spent all day yesterday making sure we had enough coffee, beans, sugar, rice, and cocoa. Today, we make tortillas. We will serve beef that has been roasted over an open fire. Then we will eat fruit for dessert. The celebration and feasting will last for days!

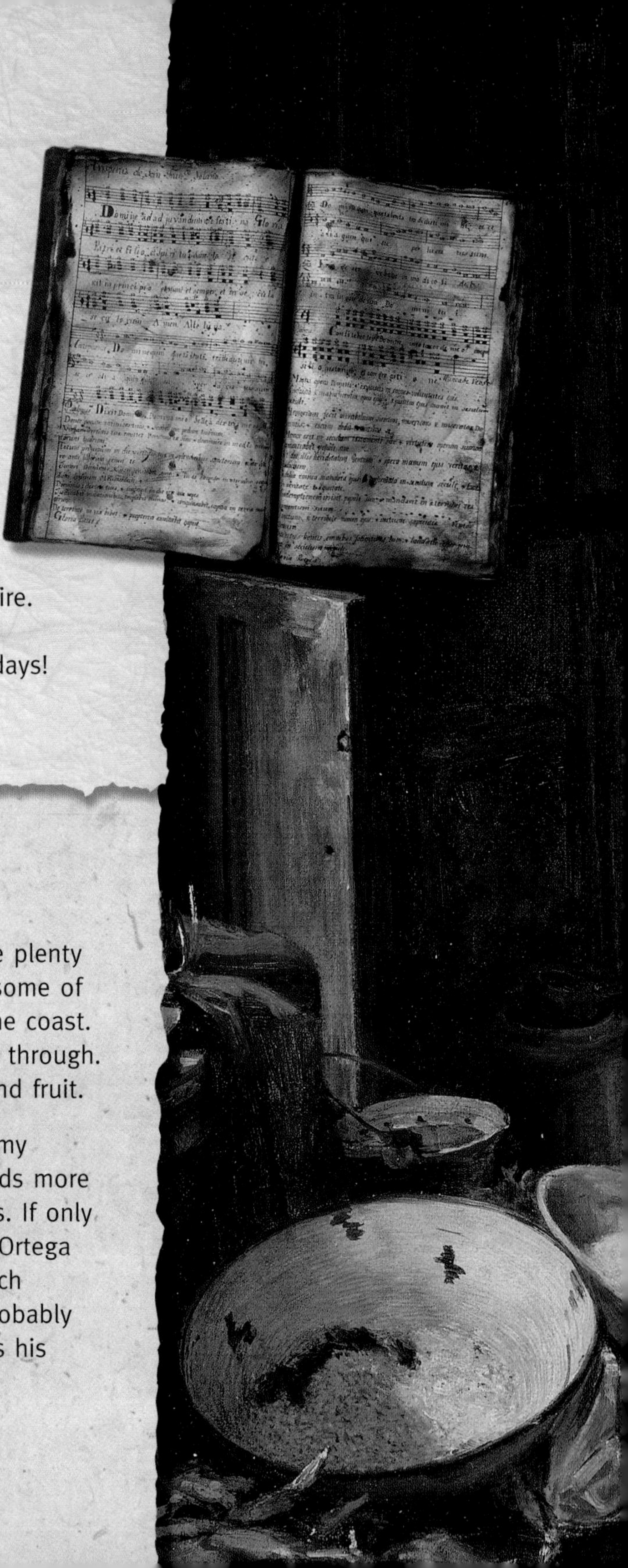

From Simón's journal
July 23, 1838

Well, the harvest is over. We will have plenty of food this next year. Papa will sell some of our flour to the Russian settlers up the coast. There are also some trappers passing through. We can sell them some of our beef and fruit.

Rosalinda has been helping me with my music for the festival. My playing needs more work, but it is not as bad as she says. If only I played as well as I ride. I hope the Ortega family will be here. I can't decide which daughter I like the most. Papa will probably decide for me. Their brother, José, has his eye on Rosalinda.

From Padre Ramón's journal

July 25, 1838

Listening to the young people sing took me back to my mission days. Ah, how I loved to teach the Indians songs! Many of their voices were beautiful. To me, when I heard the choir, it was like God shining through them. Hearing them lifting their voices in song made my heart sing. In Mexico, I work with a church choir, but somehow it is not the same as it was at the mission. Oh well, I have promised Rosalinda that I will share some stories. It will be pleasant—stories are much like songs.

A woman grinding cornmeal to make tortillas, or flatbread

From Rosalinda's diary

July 26, 1838

The dancing was wonderful. So many ranchero families were with us. I danced a fandango with José Ortega. He can do some very fancy steps. I noticed that Mama watched José and me most of the night. Later, I saw Papa talking to Señor Ortega. I wonder what my parents have planned. I am too young to marry! But he is handsome. We ate supper, and danced some more. Most of us never went to bed at all. We were very hungry again this morning. Now I am very sleepy.

From Simón's journal

July 27, 1838

Today, we played many games. I rode very well. I was able to pick up a flower from the ground as I raced past some girls. They all clapped for me. We painted our faces. We tossed eggshells filled with shredded gold and silver paper. The girls screamed and laughed as we became covered with the paper. Rosalinda throws well. She threw eggs at several of the boys riding by her. She hit them each time. We danced and sang until the sun came up.

Once the celebration was over, everyone returned to work. The Delgados had killed many cattle for the celebrations. Bones littered the field where the cattle had been slaughtered. Wild animals had already picked the bones clean. Felipe ordered his men to top the low adobe walls around the rancho with the skulls of the dead cattle. The sharp horns helped keep out wild animals and thieves.

The ranchero familes lived an outdoor life. Horses were plentiful, and nearly everyone rode. Young men rode from one rancho to another for parties. A host gave his guest a horse, and when the rider reached the next rancho he simply exchanged it for another.

Fort Ross

CHAPTER 3

Visitors Arrive

Others besides the Americans had their eyes on California. Russians began to settle in what is now Alaska in the late 1700s. They had first reached California in 1806, when a Russian ship sailed into San Francisco Bay to get food for the Alaska colony. In 1812, Russians settled north of San Francisco. Their settlement became known as Fort Ross (from a shortened version of a Russian word meaning "Russia").

The Russians at Fort Ross hunted sea otters and sold the valuable skins to China. They bought grain and meat to help supply the Alaska colony. They first got their supplies from the missions and later from the ranchos.

A Russian artist from Fort Ross was traveling around the nearby countryside. He was painting pictures of the missions and ranchos. He came to stay with the Delgado family.

From Rosalinda's diary
September 10, 1838

I am taking painting lessons! A Russian artist named Igor is staying with us. He has come from Fort Ross. The Russians there hunt seals and sea otters for their fur. Igor doesn't do that. Instead, he makes wonderful paintings of our missions and ranchos. Igor loves our bright sun and the warm brown walls of our adobe houses. We sat in the sun today, and I started to sketch the church at the presidio. When my drawing is done, I will give it to Padre Ramón.

I am learning a lot. Sometimes, I can't understand Igor's Spanish. But then he takes my hand and guides my pencil. He has bright blue eyes and a wonderful smile with very white teeth.

From Simón's journal
September 12, 1838

That Russian tells endless stories about life in the North. He says that there are many animals to trap for furs. Plus, there are tales of gold. I would like to find gold. There doesn't seem to be any in California. When Igor says that more Russians would like to move here, Papa frowns and changes the subject.

Igor eats everything in sight. They must not feed them at Fort Ross. Papa says we must give all guests as much as they want or need and even more. That is what rancheros do. It is our custom.

September 17, 1838
Alta California

My Dear Brother,

We have had several visitors at the rancho. The first and most welcome was our cousin, Padre Ramón, who was once at the Carmel Mission. He will remain with us for some months. The children are fond of him and love to hear his stories of the "old days."

We also had a Russian painter here for a few days, but he has gone. Our most recent and least welcome guest was the captain of an American ship that came to Monterey. In the spirit of California hospitality, I invited him to dinner. During the evening, the captain asked many questions about conditions here. He wanted to know how many Mexican troops were at the presidios, how much grain and beef we produced, and so on. Later on, he joked that perhaps California should become his country's 26th state. As you can imagine, I didn't smile.

Your fond brother,
Felipe

Later that night, Rosalinda and Simón begged the padre to tell them stories about the "old days." They wanted to know what life was like at the mission. Simón wanted to know if there were ever any battles. Padre Ramón began to tell a story of a time when the Indians rebelled and fled the mission. Everyone settled down to listen to his story.

The church and living quarters of a Spanish mission

CHAPTER 4

Uprising and Escape

Padre Ramón told them first what life was like for the Native Americans at the Carmel Mission. As at the other missions, the priests directed the Indians' lives. They took Indian children from their parents and raised them at the mission. The parents lived in one-story adobe houses outside the mission. The parents wanted to stay close to their children.

The men learned to make adobe bricks, tend the cattle, and work the flower and fruit gardens. Some Indian men also became woodworkers and blacksmiths. The women made clothes, wove baskets, and made pottery. Many of the Indians did not like this life. They missed their homes. They wanted to return to their villages, but the soldiers would not let them. So, the Indians rebelled. They set fire to the mission and then tried to flee.

From Simón's journal

October 8, 1838

Padre Ramón's story was exciting. The Indians first set fire to the living quarters at the mission. As the flames spread, the Indians fled over the walls. They had made rope ladders. When word reached the presidio, Papa and his soldiers raced to the mission. They were too late. Most of the Indians had escaped by then.

The padre said that Papa and his men raced up to the mission on their horses. They put out the fires and took charge of the Indians who were still there. Later, Papa led his soldiers to find the Indians who had fled.

Papa does not talk much about his days as a soldier. His swords and his old leather armor hang on the wall. I've asked him one or twice about them, but he has little to say. I'm glad Padre Ramón told me about what Papa did.

Spanish soldier's chest armor made of stiffened leather

From Padre Ramón's journal

October 8, 1838

The children loved the story. To them it was just an exciting tale. To me, it brought back sorrowful memories. I felt so foolish then. I had thought the Indians were happy. I was wrong.

From Rosalinda's diary
October 9, 1838

The padre told us that the Indians were brought back in chains. Mama said that when she went to church the next week, one of the Indians was chained to a post. Red marks covered his body. She said that after the uprising even the music at the mission sounded sad.

Though they never were meant to be, the mission settlements were a disaster for the Native Americans. Most Indians who worked at the mission were little better than slaves. When they were crowded into missions, they could not lead healthful lives. In addition, they were exposed to diseases that often killed them. Their bodies could not fight the diseases. In 1769, when the Spanish missions began, there may have been as many as 300,000 Indians in California. By the 1830s, probably a third of them had died.

CHAPTER 5

Battling the Pirates

Just like Mexico, other Latin American countries fought for freedom from Spain. One of these countries was Argentina, which became independent in 1816. Two years later, a ship from Argentina raided Monterey. The captain was Hipólito Bouchard (ee-POHL-ee-toh boo–SHARD). Bouchard and his men hoped that the Californians might be ready to revolt against Spain. Even if that plan failed, the capital of Alta California should be worth looting.

Simón and Rosalinda had heard something about a pirate raid on Monterey from their parents. Now they asked Padre Ramón to tell them the whole story.

From Simón's journal

November 16, 1838

The pirate story is the best tale that the padre has told! It happened just about this time of the year, way back in 1818. Sailors brought a rumor to Monterey that a pirate fleet was coming to attack us. The soldiers at the presidio got ready to fight. They checked their stores of gunpowder.

They cleaned the cannons so that they wouldn't misfire. They even practiced loading and unloading them. When the fight started there would be no time for mistakes. These men were ready to do battle for the honor of Spain. Papa said the days waiting for Bouchard to sail into the bay were the longest of his life!

Hipólito Bouchard

From Rosalinda's diary

November 16, 1838

It would have been so exciting to have lived here when the pirates came! The padre said that everyone at Monterey either hid their valuables or loaded them in carts and sent them inland. I wonder which of my things I would have most wanted to have saved from the pirates.

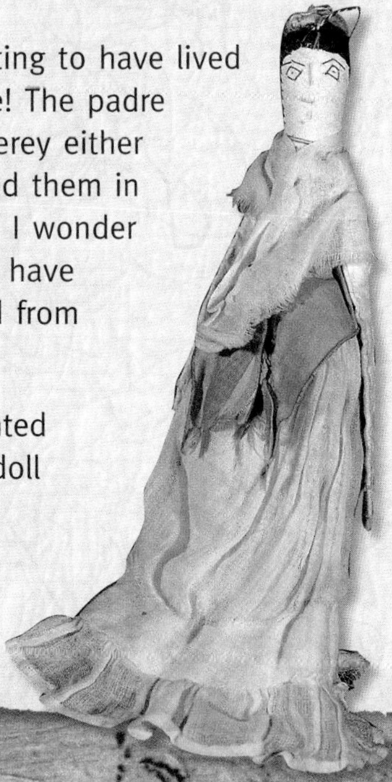

One thing I would have wanted to keep with me is my old doll that Mama gave me. It was hers when she was a girl, and I would feel terrible if anything happened to it.

From Rosalinda's diary

November 16, 1838

The padre told us how the men at the presidio watched for Bouchard's ships. In the late afternoon, they spotted two ships only five miles offshore. By midnight, one small ship was anchored less than a quarter of a mile from the fort! The soldiers shouted to them, asking them what they wanted. The pirates shouted back in English, thinking that they were fooling us. That night, both sides prepared for battle!

From Simón's journal

November 19, 1838

The padre said that by the time the sun rose, the soldiers were ready to fight. The small pirate ship remained where it was. At dawn, the pirates raised the flag of Argentina and began to fire on the fort. The soldiers returned the fire with their cannons. They hit the ship! After seven cannon shots from the presidio, the pirates lowered the flag and began to abandon ship. The soldiers of Monterey had won the battle!

From Padre Ramón's journal

November 21, 1838

The children thought the story was over when the pirates lowered their flag. But it wasn't! The next day, Bouchard and 200 men landed a short way up the coast. They wanted to avoid our cannon. Then they marched to the presidio. They had guns and a small cannon. This time, our soldiers retreated. Felipe and two men rode to the mission to warn us. I quickly sprinkled holy water in the church to protect it from these godless pirates. Then we went with the soldiers. By now, Bouchard and his men had seized the presidio. The flag of Argentina flew over Monterey. The children begged me to tell them what happened next.

From Rosalinda's diary

November 21, 1838

Padre Ramón told us how the pirates burned the houses at the presidio, but not the church or the mission. Mama smiled at the padre and said that his holy water must have worked. She and her family had packed all their valuables. They took their horses and rode into the hills when they heard the cannons firing. The first night, a mountain lion was prowling near where Mama and her family were hiding. No one slept, and Mama kept a loaded gun by her side!

The next day, Papa and a few soldiers found Mama and her family hiding in the cave where they had spent the night. Bouchard's men were still in Monterey, but they had left the mission alone. So, Papa took Mama and her family there. Padre Ramón soon joined them.

From Simón's journal

November 22, 1838

Bouchard and men stayed in Monterey five days. When Padre Ramón knew that the pirates had sailed away, he ordered that the mission bells be rung. In that way, everyone that heard them would know the danger was over.

They all rode back to the presidio. Smoke still filled the air, but the pirates were gone. They had taken whatever valuables they could find in Monterey and then burned the pueblo. Papa said it did not take long to rebuild Monterey. Then he and his soldiers raised the flag of Spain. Once again, it flew over Monterey.

Bell tower at Carmel Mission

Padre Ramón had enjoyed telling the children his tales of early mission life. Now it was time for him to return to Mexico. Before he left, there would be one more party. The governor was coming from Los Angeles to visit. In 1835, the capital of Alta California had been moved there from Monterey.

The governor wanted to see his friend Padre Ramón before the old priest left for Mexico. Felipe and his family planned a party to honor the governor. It would be a time for them all to say goodbye to Padre Ramón.

CHAPTER 6

The Governor Visits

The Delgados were proud that the governor was coming to call at the rancho. Felipe chose a fast and beautiful horse as a gift for their guest. It was cream-colored, with a silver-white mane and tail. Simón and Rosalinda looked forward to impressing the governor with their riding. The days flew by as they prepared for the governor's arrival.

From Rosalinda's diary

December 10, 1838

Mama and I are filling the house with flowers. I have been polishing silver, sweeping, and helping Mama clean. She said that the house must shine. I think that it does.

I have been taking drinks to the workers who are helping us get ready for the governor's visit. Some Americans are coming to the party. I will practice my English with them. I wonder if more Americans will move here.

From Simón's journal

December 11, 1838

The governor arrives today. Papa says that since the governor moved the capital to Los Angeles there are more people settling there.

I want to work for the governor, so I am learning French and English. Papa says I had better make sure my English is good. He fears the Americans will take over Alta California. I wonder if he is right. I would hate to lose our rancho.

From Padre Ramón's journal

December 13, 1838

Tomorrow I leave Alta California—probably forever. I think back on my years at the mission. I see now that our work with the Indians failed. We did not understand them. They did not want our way of life. But the missions did help settle Alta California. We did teach the Indians some skills, even if few use them now. We cannot undo the past. Who knows what the future holds? I wonder how people will remember the missions. I'm glad now that I told the children my stories.

I think things will continue to change here. I see so many people I do not know. I fear our old Spanish ways will be lost as more outsiders settle here. Felipe and his family will endure. They are strong and proud.

Carmel Mission in the 1800s

Epilogue

The people of Monterey rebuilt their pueblo in less than four months. Felipe and Maria stayed on their rancho and continued to work it. Their children moved away. Simón worked first for the Mexican government. Then, using his English skills, he worked for the United States when California became a state in 1850. He and his family lived in the new capital.

San Francisco's harbor in 1850

Rosalinda married a settler who had journeyed West from Illinois. They moved north to San Francisco and started a **vineyard** with grapevines that had first been grown at the mission.

As he feared, Padre Ramón never returned to California. He continued to teach singing, which gave him great joy. The padre listened to his choir and remembered the mission church. The music took him back to his early days in Alta California.

Glossary

adobe – made from mud bricks that are baked in the sun

bay – a part of a sea extending into the land

custom – a traditional way of doing things

mission – a settlement that included a church, living quarters, and farmlands

presidio – a fort established by the Spanish to protect their missions

pueblo – a village or community

rancho – a ranch, or farm, in the Spanish Southwest

vineyard – a place planted with grapevines